Lungs

Lisa Greathouse

Consultant

Gina Montefusco, RN
Children's Hospital Los Angeles
Los Angeles, California

Publishing Credits

Dona Herweck Rice, *Editor-in-Chief*; Lee Aucoin, *Creative Director*; Don Tran, *Print Production Manager*; Timothy J. Bradley, *Illustration Manager*; Chris McIntyre, *Editorial Director*; James Anderson, *Associate Editor*; Jamey Acosta, *Associate Editor*; Jane Gould, *Editor*; Peter Balaskas, *Editorial Administrator*; Neri Garcia, *Senior Designer*; Stephanie Reid, *Photo Editor*; Rachelle Cracchiolo, M.S.Ed., *Publisher*

Image Credits

cover Sadeugra/Shutterstock; p.1 Sadeugra/Shutterstock; p.4 (left) Pathathai Chungyam/Dreamstime, (right) Jaren Wicklund/iStockphoto; p.5 (left) Carmen Martínez Banús/iStockphoto, (top right) Joshua Hodge Photography/iStockphoto, (bottom right) Michelle D. Milliman/Shutterstock; p.6 Ansar80/Atanas Bozhikov/Shutterstock; p.7 Andriy Petrenko/iStockphoto; p.8 Davi Sales Batista/Shutterstock; p.9 Felix Mizioznikov/Shutterstock; p.10 (left) Andreas Gradin/Shutterstock, (right) Miroslaw Pieprzyk/iStockphoto; p.11 Steve Cole/iStockphoto; p.12 Juriah Mosin/Shutterstock; p.13 (top) Jeff64/Dreamstime, (bottom) Robert Dant/iStockphoto; p.14 (left) Charles Daghlian/Wikimedia, (right) Oguz Aral/Shutterstock; p.15 Kirill Kurashov/Algecireño/Shutterstock; p.16 (left) Mikulich Alexander Andreevich/Shutterstock, (right) Natalya Kozyreva/iStockphoto; p.17 Andrea Danti/Shutterstock; p.18 Michelangelus/Shutterstock; p.19 Sebastian Kaulitzki/Shutterstock; p.20 Sadeugra/Shutterstock; p.21 Erna Vader/iStockphoto; p.22 Sebastian Kaulitzki/Shutterstock; p.23 (top) Rob Marmion/Shutterstock, (right) Christopher P. Grant/Shutterstock; p.24 (top) iofoto/Shutterstock, (bottom) Zurijeta/Shutterstock; p.25 Andrea Danti/Shutterstock; p.26 (left) Angel_Vasilev77/Shutterstock, (right) Shariff Che' Lah/Dreamstime; p.27 Monkey Business Images/Shutterstock; p.28 Rocket400 Studio/Shutterstock; p.29 Ana Clark; p.32 Dr. Pierre Massion

Teacher Created Materials

5301 Oceanus Drive
Huntington Beach, CA 92649-1030
http://www.tcmpub.com

ISBN 978-1-4333-1431-5
©2011 Teacher Created Materials, Inc.
Printed in China

Table of Contents

Staying Alive

You do it every time you take a step, throw a ball, or just say hello. You do not even think about it.

What is it? It is breathing, of course!

You need to breathe to stay alive. Many parts of your body work together so you can breathe.

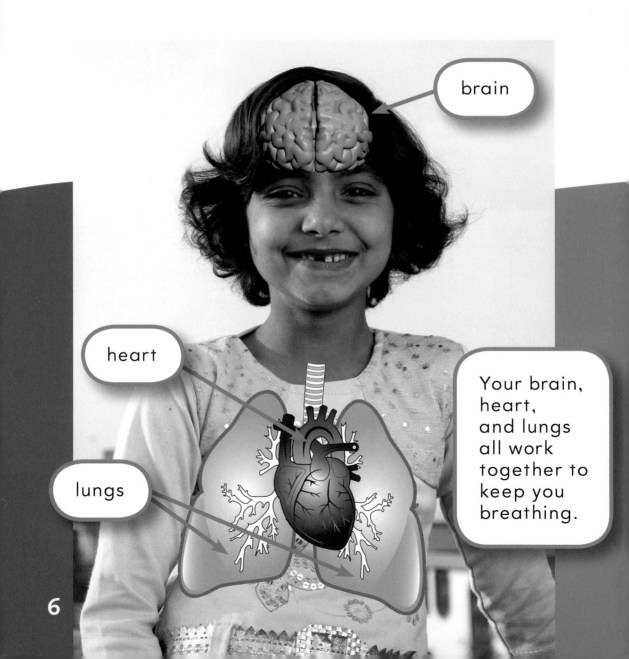

brain

heart

lungs

Your brain, heart, and lungs all work together to keep you breathing.

But, you could not get air in your body without your lungs!

Fun Fact

Your lungs are pink and squishy—like a sponge!

Breathe in. Your chest gets bigger.
Breathe out. Your chest gets smaller.
That is because your lungs are in there.

You have two lungs. Your heart is between them.

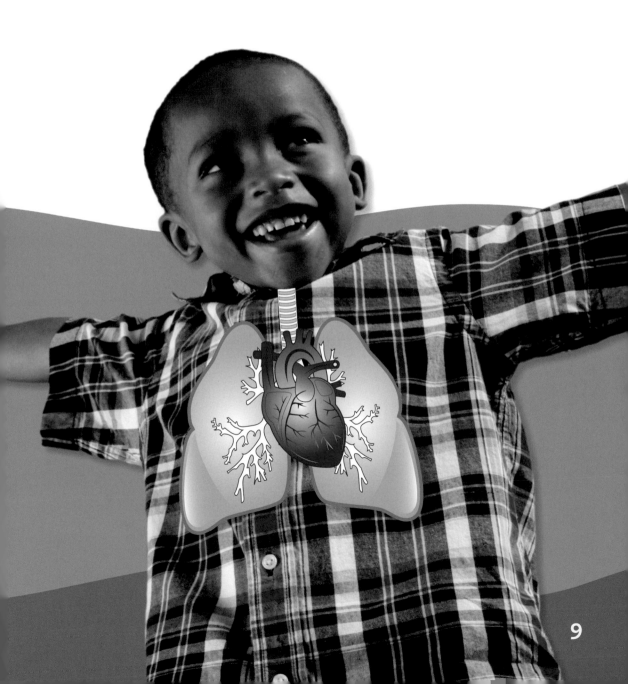

You breathe about 20 times each minute. You breathe faster when your body works harder, like when you run.

Where does the air go after you breathe it in?

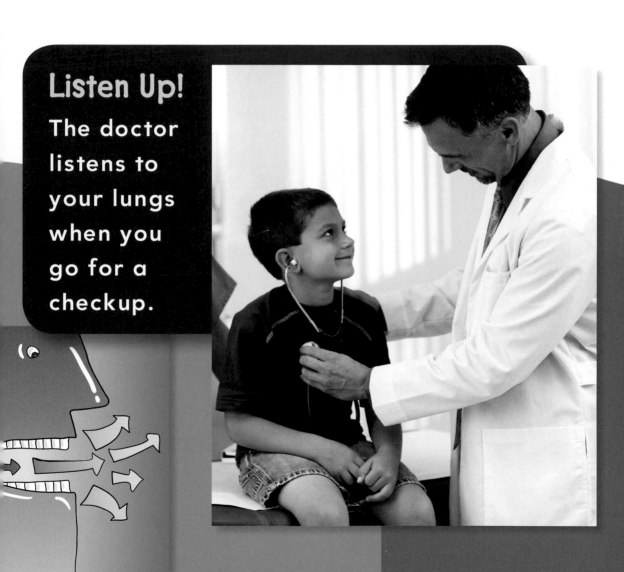

Listen Up!
The doctor listens to your lungs when you go for a checkup.

Breathing

Your nose does more than just smell!
Your nose takes in air when you **inhale**.

Sticky hairs in your nose clean the air as it goes by. What do you think about that?

nose hairs

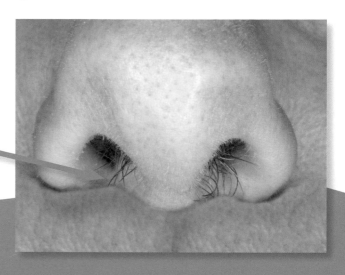

Next, the air goes to your **windpipe**. The windpipe is a tube in your neck. The tube is long.

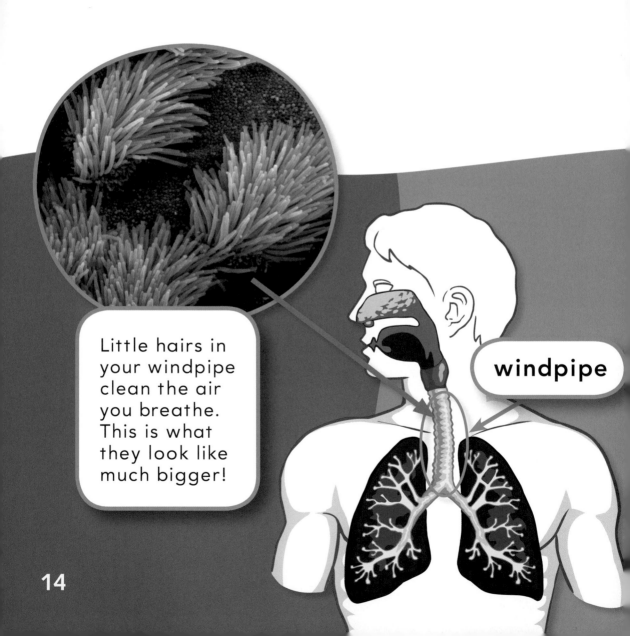

Little hairs in your windpipe clean the air you breathe. This is what they look like much bigger!

windpipe

Your windpipe also helps clean the air before it gets to your lungs.

There is **oxygen** (OK-si-juhn) in the air that you breathe.

Your lungs and heart work to send the oxygen to **cells** all over your body. The oxygen keeps you alive!

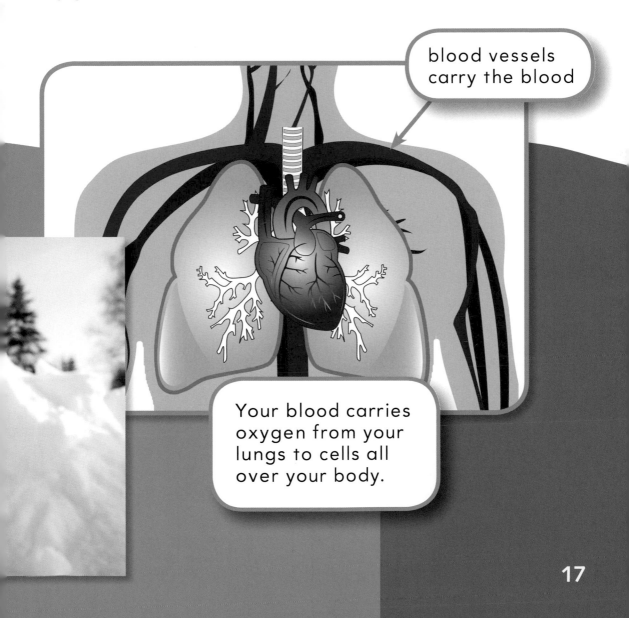

blood vessels carry the blood

Your blood carries oxygen from your lungs to cells all over your body.

But the oxygen does not just float in your body. It takes a ride in your blood!

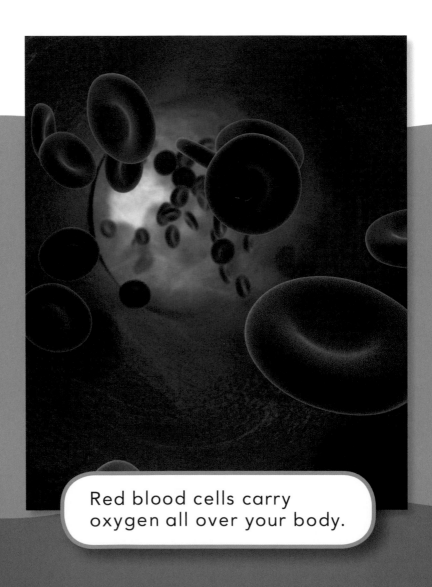

Red blood cells carry oxygen all over your body.

Your heart pumps that blood to all the cells in your body.

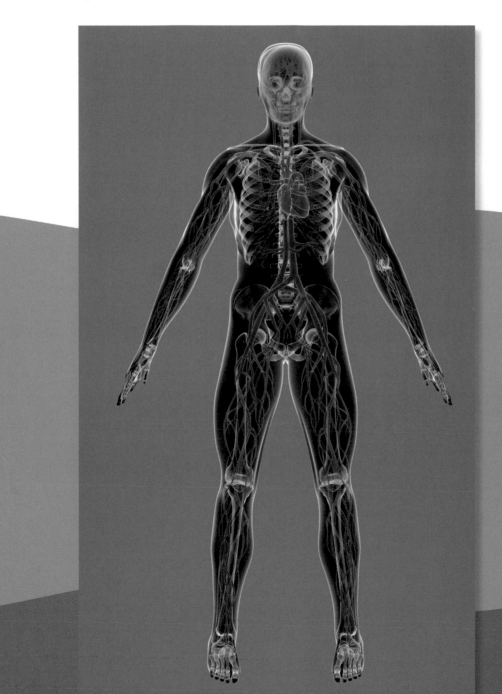

Breathe in. Then, breathe out.

When you breathe out, your lungs get rid of waste from your cells.

Your Brain Is the Boss

How do you know when to take a breath? Your brain does that! It gives orders to your lungs.

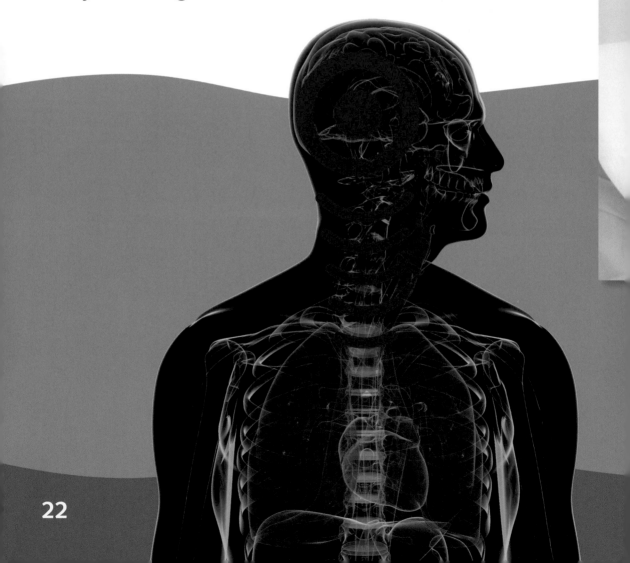

Your brain does that even when you are asleep.

How Many Cups?

Each breath is about a cupful of air. You breathe in and out more than 2,000 gallons of air each day!

It takes a lot of muscle for your lungs to pump air in and out all the time.

That is what the **diaphragm** (DY-uh-fram) is for. It works nonstop!

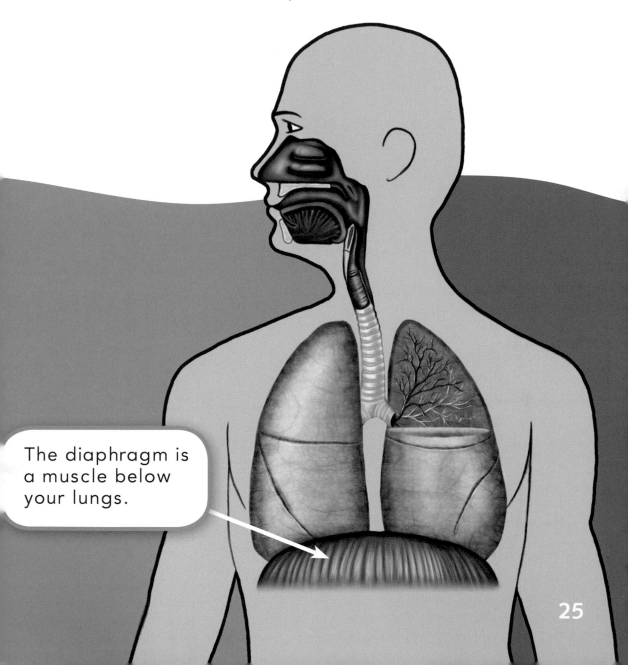

The diaphragm is a muscle below your lungs.

Keep Your Lungs Healthy

Now you know why you need healthy lungs. Take good care of them!

It is best *never* to smoke. And keep active to help your lungs stay in shape.

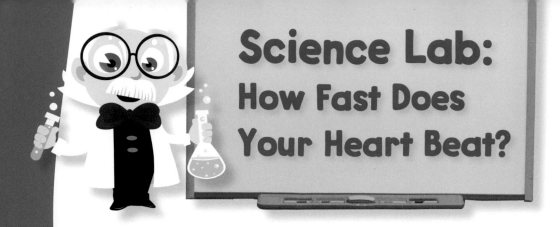

Science Lab: How Fast Does Your Heart Beat?

How much faster does your heart beat when you exercise? Find your pulse and see!

Materials:

- clock or watch with a second hand for each group of students

Procedure:

❶ Use your index and middle fingers to find your pulse on the inside of your other wrist or the side of your neck.

❷ Count the number of beats in 15 seconds.

❸ Multiply that number by four to find out how many times your heart beats in one minute. Ask a grown-up if you need help.

❹ Write down your "at rest" heartbeat.

❺ Run in place or do jumping jacks for two minutes.

❻ Stop and check your pulse again.

❼ Repeat steps 1–3. Write down your "active" heart rate.

❽ Subtract your "at rest" heart rate from your "active" heart rate. The difference is how many more times your heart beats per minute when you exercise.

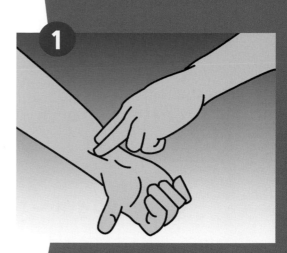

Glossary

cells—the building blocks of your body

diaphragm—the muscle that pumps air in and out of your lungs

inhale—breathing in

oxygen—a gas you need to breathe

windpipe—tube in your neck that carries air to the lungs

Index

A Scientist Today

Dr. Pierre Massion studies how cancer grows in the lungs. He also studies ways to find the cancer early so that we can cure it.